In *blood on the map of man*, Scott Ferry offers an extended meditation that is at once intimate, philosophical, and profoundly ecological. This book-length poem transforms the ordinary—parenting, illness, yard work, grief—into a luminous field of inquiry where the personal and the universal continually intertwine. Ferry's voice is precise yet fluid, attentive to both lyric image and ethical weight. Domestic moments become sites of metaphysical resonance: a child's Lego dinosaur embodies evolutionary imagination, a dermatologist's cauterization echoes mortality's inscription on the flesh, a daughter's lament for "a human body" gestures toward exile from the numinous.

What makes this sequence extraordinary is its patience and scope. Each section accrues like a meditation bead, building a work that resists despair by locating fragile moments of grace: a father laughing with his children, the shimmer of river light, the possibility of solidarity even against mortality. *blood on the map of man* is an ambitious and luminous contribution to contemporary poetry—a sustained act of witness reminding us of the porous boundary between loss and wonder.

I recommend this book to every reader of poetry, but especially to those with families, who will recognize in its pages the profound beauty, vulnerability, and transcendence found in the daily fabric of love.

-Rick Christiansen, author of *Not a Hero*

Scott Ferry's newest collection blends care and worry as Ferry raises each poem with the patience and tenderness with which he raises his children. *blood on the map of man* thrives under the same truth and sunlight Ferry shines on the garden in Winter. These words were developed in darkness, but each Scott Ferry poem is worth a thousand photographs.

>-Shawnte Orion, author of *The Existential Cookbook* (NYQ Books)

blood on the map of man

a poem

scott ferry

Luchador Press
Big Tuna, TX

Copyright © Scott Ferry 2026
First Edition: 1 3 5 7 9 10 8 6 4 2
ISBN: 979-8-89975-024-3
LCCN: 2026934558

Author photo: Scott Ferry
Cover image: Lani Ferry
Title page image: Scott Ferry

All rights reserved. No part of this publication may be reproduced or transmitted in any form or by any means, electronic or mechanical, including photocopying, recording or by info retrieval system, without prior written permission from the author.

Acknowledgments:

Four Feathers: "16"
Heavy Feather: "2, 4, 7, 19, 21"
MacQueen's Quinterly: "11"
Meat For Tea: "12, 25"
ONE ART: "1, 26"
Thimble: "6"

Table of Contents:

sometimes the kitchen cleans itself / 1

the dermatologist looks over my skin / 2

i search my grave— / 3

the apple blossoms are the same color white / 4

sun behind / 5

when my daughter feels good about herself / 6

find a dead crow on my lawn / 7

sometimes the nostalgia overwhelms me / 8

my usual walk along the duwamish river / 9

my son says if a megalodon was alive / 10

my daughter weeps to my wife / 11

in the dream / 13

i help my son refold a paper airplane / 14

i have always been seeking something

   i have lost / 15

i am 26— / 16

i tell my son we need to get out of the pool / 18

all of my father's skis / 19

my son tells me about his dream / 20

i kill a colony of ants today / 21

my son wakes up weeping / 22

in the dream a woman / 23

on my usual walk by the puget sound / 25

i sift the april air / 26

the night after my son has his nightmare / 27

physicists say that everything is
    happening now / 28

my son spends two hours at the beach / 29

my daughter is burdened / 31

in the dream / 32

i haven't written about my heart / 33

my daughter tries to inhale deeply
    and she coughs / 34

*Flesh covers the bone
and the flesh searches
for more than flesh.*

-Charles Bukowski

To Lani and Ryland

blood on the map of man

1.

sometimes the kitchen cleans itself
the shower shines white as the prayers of clouds

i look around and there are no grievances
even god's nametag is crisp

and i take a breath and wait
another breath and wait

i don't trust the sky to
hold

2.

the dermatologist looks over my skin
to see if something dead has boiled up
from under the surface
                      a rusted car with intact remains

or if something has been branded
into my hide by ultraviolet
by hate and cruelty
                      dried blood on the map of man

he burns off damage with ice
before it grows its own body inside mine
before the child inside
                      is hijacked

i have enough skin i think
to grow back any voice
any voice i have saved
                      from the fire

3.

i search my grave—
raspberry and rugosa
blanket the stone

my children's children's children
reach roots through
soil

my shoes sing to the bees
my ashes tremble in the silt
my eyelashes curl in the wind

and all of the soft parts of me
still purr inside the vines
inside the feral

chambers of the
earth

4.

the apple blossoms are the same color white
as the grubs which are destroying my lawn

i take a photo of the diaphanous white flesh
of the flower against the blue blood of the sky

i furiously claw out the decaying earth
and uncover each curled alabaster larvae

i ask my son to get gloves on, to help me throw
each transparent insect in the bin

he says that he can see their eyes
he says he can see their hearts and blue blood

each grub would have grown into a flying thing
my son handles them gently as he discards them

there is nothing as white as death
nothing as bloody as birth

i share the image of wings in the light
i bury the blind in the dark

5.

sun behind
our shadows reach in front of us

my son's darkness is unintentional
and mine is merely a function of lost magic

light reaches inside our bodies and spills
out our flat poltergeists—legs stretching

my hands protecting the light slowly waning
his hands projecting out from his fingers

a tiny god with every power
in his name

6.

when my daughter feels good about herself
she radiates a sad sweetness—

a cherry blossom opening
under wind thrashing and uncalm words

she has been here all along
under a mirror black sea

singing clear obsidian—
weeping dark salt

in her sleep

7.

find a dead crow on my lawn
there is nothing poetic about it

i put on a glove a carry it to where
i will remember to put it in the trash

my son pokes at it wants to save its skeleton
i say no we do not know how it died

and promptly bring him inside to wash his hands
i don't want to think it is a bad omen

but i fear it is—so i resist mythologizing
the death of a messenger of death

on the earth directly in front
of my feet

8.

sometimes the nostalgia overwhelms me
even for moments that are still happening

my son constructing a dinosaur that never existed
out of legos with hinged neck and 20 feet of skull

named prionostrosaurus he shows me how it moves
and his mother helps him adapt the hinge

so the head doesn't swing all the way down
i realize that this scene mixing with the laughs

and rain on the skylights will be gone soon
and i will be ninety years old wishing to be here again

with all of the love washing through us
like sudden floods

9.

my usual walk along the duwamish river
and i stop to look into the water

not wanting anything
the reflections of silver cobalt lemon

overlapping bodies feather into currents
connecting the whole of my breath

the blood of the sky upended into veins
and tidal valves stretching along where flesh

and spirit coalesce and blur
my sea also wind-written

in flashes of sharp
sun

10.

my son says if a megalodon was alive
it would be bigger than the whole ocean!

i say no, but they are big
he thinks and says if all the people in the world

jumped into the ocean and swam together
like a megalodon it would be bigger than a megalodon!

and i added and it would scare
away the megalodon!

he agreed and made a triumphant harrrrhhhg!
with his fist out

i am encouraged that he realizes the power
we have when we are united

embracing and side stroking through the blank
and bottomless sea

our languages enervating this great silver body
our stories cradling everyone within

this great silver skin

11.

my daughter weeps to my wife
says that she feels trapped in a human body

that she is supposed to be moon or a star
that she doesn't belong here

i ask her later and she says the hate
and the negativity are too much

that she doesn't see the point
of all the pain and suffering

i explain i have always felt this way
and that many many many people do

some try to escape it by killing themselves
some find the fun and pleasure in this world

so why not? i say eat your favorite foods
listen to your favorite music

i explain it really helped me to find a way to help
i say to find out why you are here

i know that my writing is what i can give back
i say to her your art and poetry

are natural to you maybe that is the way
you help this world

i feel her settle and say
so this life is all a simulation?

like a field trip?
i don't know for sure but i think so i answer.

but you are here now
so you might as well find your joy here

and your people, my daughter
there are plenty of us in exile

sharing sparks in the
darkness

12.

in the dream
i have to run to make the train
because my fourteen children are all there

i even know that i don't really run
anymore (knee replacement)
yet i sprint across

the lawn jump benches slalom through people
and i keep waiting for my legs to hurt
but they don't

and when i burst into the train all my children
cheer and welcome me with
my own young

face

13.

i help my son refold a paper airplane
to make the lines straighter
and add a paper clip to the back
because it keeps diving

when we go to the playground
he throws it over a hundred times
from the top of the slide
from the edge of the web structure

from a sunny hill
and most times it doesn't go far
barrels into the ground
smashing the cockpit

so he spends some time
uncrushing it before he throws it again
he finds joy in any amount of flight
even a rapid boomerang back to his feet

i think this kid will do ok here
on this planet
reshaping his psyche after a hundred falls
running back up the hill

like he has never been
hurt

14.

i have always been seeking something i have lost
a place of light without pain
if i take apart each of my molecules
it is there—the burn and hum of god's wet fabric

when i grasp it it sheds its skin
when i name it it makes all words hiss as the tide retreats
if i listen it rolls like a warm static
under my lids

if i go towards it i go farther in or farther under
i speak to it like a bodiless voice in a hall
it doesn't make anything easier
really

i still have this mask and script
and theater full of physics
but i wish on what is everything within everything
to at least heal what can be healed

share it with my wife my children
eat it in the april sun—
an asterisk on the wide water
a birdthroat in the sky

15.

i am 26—
my words break and fall

can't speak to humans
hold my body together with insomnia

shake on my mother's couch
my first career a slow failure

ask god or a future version
of myself for help

i listen—cold dialtone
a vague ache

you will eventually know
something says

and when i look back i know not to reach
across time and comfort myself

this is the 40 days in the desert
gilgamesh's 12 days of darkness

the whale's acidic stomach
there are reasons

to slaughter yourself and weep
which are not known

to those who slaughter themselves
and weep

and have i emerged?
at 55?

i have some ash written
on ash i can show you

i can sing a clear song
in the night

16.

i tell my son we need to get out of the pool
but, of course, he wants to stay
as i crawl along the shallow water to the exit
i feel his tiny but strong hand grip my ankle

and i let him begin to move my large body backwards
i see time flash through the blur
as if i am getting younger
the deeper he pulls me

after he has transported me all the way back
to the barrier between earth and ether
i stand up and look surprised
i am five again with him

a brother or a grinning father
it is impossible to tell
and we dart and splash and dive
in the eternal light

when it is time for me to go
hopefully many years from now
i will tell him i must go alone
that he will not be able to pull me back

but share this with your children, son
be young with them in this grand sparkling pool
for the time you have
which is forever

17.

all of my father's skis
are leaning up against the walls of the old condo
along with boots and many 1970s orange parkas
leather gloves bags socks all seeming too new

i think he left these for me but none of them fit
like too-long sentences that would break my legs
his laugh intonation way of charming
none of them are mine

there is a reason i left them all here
and i think how would i get them
out of the dream
anyhow?

18.

my son tells me about his dream
that we were at the nothing birthday party
or the everything birthday party
mom and leilani were also there

who's birthday was it?
everyone's! he replies
and the party went all the way into
space

what were we doing?
swimming around
dad you know in space
you can swim around in the air?

was there food?
ice cream!
i have the feeling he is explaining
the afterlife or the beforelife

but i don't mention that
i just say how cool!
can we get up now dad?
yes son

and i carry him to the couch
on my shoulders wrap him
in a womb-like blanket
wait for life to begin

19.

i kill a colony of ants today
poison on a countertop
sticking tiny bodies
together

queen somewhere under
the house slowly dying
as her dutiful servants
feed her forbidden

names

20.

my son wakes up weeping
says he can't talk about his dream yet
as my wife and i hold him

he finally explains between short breaths
that it started with grizzlies and lemmings
then spiderman came

and more spidermen
and they started killing everyone
my wife says how scary! how horrible!

and we embrace him until the breaths get
longer and quieter and i ask if he can
help me make french toast

french toast french toast i repeat
he bonks me softly on the head and
says i don't want face toast!

face toast? and we spend the next
few minutes splatting pretend face toast
on each other's bodies

but through the laughter i feel sad that his heroes
have already begun betraying him
interrupting his trust

with webs of blood

21.

in the dream a woman
kept choosing people to torture
or even kill in the room we waited in

each person was mutilated without sound
or complaint like they were
on the news

each victim stood up and succumbed as if
they were compelled by duty and i just got angrier
and began cursing where i sat

none of my cohorts seemed to care
that people were being slaughtered
and admonished me for resisting

the woman came next for a young sickly girl
and i stood up and said no no take me you
sick fucker don't you dare take her

and i kept screaming what is wrong with you?
why are you doing this? and all the remaining
people in the room, the soon to be sacrificed,

were appalled i was speaking up
again i asked the woman why she was murdering
these innocent people and she replied

it is a beautiful thing when done gracefully sir
and i kept thinking she was going to make
me kneel and begin cutting off my ears

but she didn't she stood there stunned
because i was getting in the way of her job
i was the difficult customer

but the girl and her mother gave me a weak
smile and i continued to shout and stomp around
wondering why i was there

why no one was angry

22.

on my usual walk by the puget sound
and i see a large canadian goose flying
towards me and then i realize it isn't veering off

but targeting me staring at me mouth open
with its barbed pink tongue flashing like a siren
i keep thinking it will fly up or away but no

i have to pillbug into myself to escape being hit
and i turn around and the bird is a winged demon
belching ancient threats to all

who would steal its eggs
i walk away as calmly as i can
making my body as small and transparent

as wind as winter-worn leaves
my steps ghosts on gravel
my spirit a hidden sea

23.

i sift the april air
        with my fingers
                hoping to catch
                          the light

24.

the night after my son has his nightmare
he shakes in bed trying to burrow into me
he says he doesn't want to sleep
he doesn't want to dream

i distract him knowing the cliff he is on the edge of
i ask about pets can we have a wolf as a pet?
all dogs are wolves but dogs can't talk he says
well they know words we say to them

what else talks besides humans?
whales dolphins parrots crows
crows don't talk he replies
i say there is a story of a man who raised a crow

and it began to talk and it would fly
to the elementary school and go through the window
and talk to the children
and even curse (but i don't tell him that)

and he begins speaking in crow language
we have a discussion not an argument
in corvid and he steps back from the abyss
guided by the tongue of a black bird

in his shiny red throat

25.

physicists say that everything is happening now
as if all of the dramas and blood are starflakes
made from a chimpanzee typing
hamlet in a roomless
room

i am sometimes the primate clicking keys
sometimes hamlet poor yoricking
sometimes ophelia translating the river
sometimes polonius knifed through the veil
and always the ghost of them all

ruing in the wings

26.

my son spends two hours at the beach
collecting body parts of dead crabs
i let him drift down the coast
as long as i can still see him
and i become a thing that sits
and stares at the water

the wind stops and the puget sound
becomes a white mirror
people and birds flick along
like sputtering fuses
my heart an open conduit
of brine and lost time

my son comes and reports
all of his discoveries the sharp footed crab leg
the ancient jaw of an extinct shrimp
a guarding claw or a killing claw
the fossil of a sea scorpion
the mouth pieces that slice

i don't usually let time go like this
so i slowly gather it pull him from the devonian age
place all the skeletons into a bigger skeleton
he is not yet a being of the clock
so he transverses the river
his feet dappled light in a stream

of light all going toward the sound
and refilling spilling refilling
us transporting our brittle bones
against a current for a flash of
silver through the roots and a hand to
hold on the way back home

27.

my daughter is burdened
by the moon— it scrapes
her insides like barnacles
on wrists

the moon doesn't know
that it pulls all the blood
from her as the shadows
gain purchase

the fairness of god
is perpetually sacrosanct—
but not the moon
if it is governed at all

i prepare slaughtered cow
my wife boils bone broth
to replace what is
shed

her body's gravid repletion
the loss as it sloughs
the pain as the uterus tries to keep
what the moon always takes

i see her straining against gravity
her body shaking against
the cold bulk
of dust

28.

in the dream
i am naked and then notice room service
i pull on some shorts and see the huge pile
of dirty laundry on my floor

next i see the flies circling the room
there must be a hundred
all different sizes and murmurating
like breaths of smoke

i try to corral them squeeze them against the wall
but they squirt and flow like pepper
the maid looks at my dead elephant of clothes
and me chasing grey ghosts around the room

with a piece of cardboard
i point to the flies as if this is her fault
that she should dispose of them
she gives me this look which says

i don't interfere with people's shadows
and pushes her cart past my doorway
with disgust and
haste

29.

i haven't written about my heart
my real heart as it hides—
a reflection of a greywhite wing

all of the places have been hurt
and the glass has been set
sky against sea

i weep sometimes that i cannot be
all that i want to be for god
for my children for my wife for all of you

there are so many ashen gates around me
the april rain falls but never touches me
i have written what i can share

my script a seagull on a cold mirror
the hanzi for ocean has nine lines
my heart has four holes

bathed in silver halides
what is exposed to light is burned
in the skin a simple curl of a snake

a tendon a finger held in the dark
as the wash of sleep
pours in

30.

my daughter tries to inhale deeply and she coughs
tells the doctor her asthma is ok
he says in a comical way don't lie to me
you can barely breathe

after the nebulizer she is more relaxed face flushed red
her doctor tells us she has influenza a
there is a reason she feels terrible
somehow the diagnosis makes it easier

words for gasping are definable
can be written and understood
and how many times in her life
will she be air starved and will the labels help?

she writes poems which are more like prayers
about the thoughts which strangle her
once the words are on the paper
she can breathe

she is proud of her poems
her way of taking that which chokes her
and stretching the red bronchioles
into strips of song

the elastic opening and the darkness flying out
each syllable a sweet clot
each line a way to dissolve
the cage

Scott Ferry did not choose this. Mostly he has been forced into writing by various spirit contracts, many of which he has not honored in the last 2.3 million years. When he got here to this planet, he thought it was all some type of mistake, a missed exit on the wormhole (a view he daughter also holds). It could be worse, he would tell you, and he may show you a photograph of a dewdrop on a web or tell you about that one steak place that you can sizzle your meat on a hot stone or just say the word "coffee." Although he has written many books of poetry which have all garnered meager attention, he does keep poeting and hoping his words find a few shiny outcasts and give them hope. His most important work is fathering, husbanding, and acting as a RN for our Veterans. His most recent books are *Sapphires on the Graves* (Glass Lyre 2024), *500 Hidden Teeth* (Meat For Tea 2024), and *dear tiny flowers* (Sheila-Na-Gig 2025). More of his work is @ ferrypoetry.com.

This project was made possible, in part, by generous support from the Osage Arts Community.

Osage Arts Community provides temporary time, space and support for the creation of new artistic works in a retreat format, serving creative people of all kinds — visual artists, composers, poets, fiction and nonfiction writers. Located on a 152-acre farm in an isolated rural mountainside setting in Central Missouri and bordered by ¾ of a mile of the Gasconade River, OAC provides residencies to those working alone, as well as welcoming collaborative teams, offering living space and workspace in a country environment to emerging and mid-career artists. For more information, visit us at www.osageac.org

www.ingramcontent.com/pod-product-compliance
Lightning Source LLC
LaVergne TN
LVHW041638070526
838199LV00052B/3435